Seasons of the Crane

by Dale Stahlecker
and Martin Frentzel

Illustrations by LisaBeth Daly

Heritage Associates, Inc.
P.O. Box 6291
Albuquerque, New Mexico 87197

First Edition

Cover by LisaBeth Daly

Design by Peter Manchester
Typography by Prototype

ISBN 0-910467-07-2
Library of Congress Catalog Card No. pending

Contents

Foreword

Sandhill and whooping cranes have been the subject of thousands of printed pages in scientific journals and books. But little has been written on this topic for the interested lay reader. Dale Stahlecker and Martin Frentzel have combined their talents as biologist-ecologist and popular-style writer to produce this stimulating book about two of America's most fascinating birds. The authors' experience with cranes and their habitat provide the know-how that transfers readers into the scenes described. One can feel the biting wind along the Texas coast and see migrating cranes silhouetted against darkening skies over New Mexico. This book fulfills the need for a scientifically accurate, popular-style text that the general public can enjoy.

—Dr. James Lewis
Whooping Crane Coordinator
United States Fish and Wildlife Service

Introduction

It was a snowy, cold Thanksgiving Day, but about midafternoon the sun poked through the clouds as the storm continued moving east toward the Sangre de Cristo Mountains.

The trails at Bandelier National Monument were muddy from the light, melting snow. Two hikers, with frosty breath and crimson cheeks, stood atop a mesa and stared toward the east and the Rio Grande. In this quiet part of the world so near the laboratories of Los Alamos, where the nuclear age was born a few decades earlier, an ancient tradition was being reenacted.

Somewhere in the distance, a flight of sandhill cranes was winging its way south for the winter. The hikers could hear them, but try as they might they could not locate the clamoring birds. The sky above, where the cranes are usually seen from these mesa tops, was void of the migrants. But out over the Rio Grande, it seemed, a large flock was making its annual journey from the north.

What a strange day to be flying. The sky had been dark almost all day, and even now, toward the east, gray sheets of rain or snow continued to fall.

At last a bird came into view. It broke out from behind a black cloud, moving with strong, steady wingbeats. It was only the leader. Within minutes 100 or more birds had flown one-by-one through the break in the clouds and continued in the path flown by the birds before them. In just a few minutes they were gone. Another cloud consumed them, and once again the hikers were alone on a dreary November day.

Slowly the cranes' music receded. The cranes became a memory, a memory which would spark deep admiration for birds so strong they continue their migration through the first snowstorm of the year.

Where had these cranes come from? Where were they going? How do they live? These questions and many more are asked each year as people see the migrating cranes. Where can I see them? For how long?

The intent of this book is to provide crane watchers with some basic information about the habits of sandhill and whooping cranes. It is written about the cranes that winter in New Mexico and Texas. Both of these states have whooping cranes, an endangered species which has migrated across the North American continent for at least two million years. There are also thousands of sandhill cranes in those states, some of which travel from the Arctic to the Southwest and back again each year.

Cranes as a group were among the earliest birds to evolve. They appeared in the Eocene, 65 million years ago. Whooping crane fossils have been found among Pleistocene deposits.

Seasons of the Crane is an effort to explain the lives of cranes to the thousands of people who enjoy their voices and their stately beauty.

This book would not have been possible without the information gathered through the tireless efforts of crane biologists throughout the United States and Canada. Because of their efforts, sandhill cranes still prosper and whooping cranes are climbing back from near extinction.

This book shares information on cranes that has appeared in many scientific papers. Of particular value have been the reports of Robert Porter Allen, Tom Stehn, Frank Johnson,

Mary Bishop, and David Blankinship on whooping cranes at Aransas National Wildlife Refuge in Texas. Ernie Kuyt's works on whooping cranes at Wood Buffalo National Park were also very useful. For information on the Rocky Mountain sandhill cranes and fostered whooping cranes, the scientific papers and reports of Rod Drewien have been invaluable. So too, have been numerous conversations and visits with him over the last several years. Since much of his work is as yet unpublished, we appreciate his willingness to share information that has helped to make this book complete.

Jim Lewis, Whooping Crane Coordinator for the U.S. Fish and Wildlife Service, was very cooperative, particularly in providing up-to-date information on whooping cranes and by allowing the use of his extensive library of crane books, reports, and proceedings from scientific meetings. He also reviewed several drafts of this book.

Photographs used by the artist were provided by the U.S. Fish and Wildlife Service, Jim Karo, Bruce Halstead, Steve Hoffman, and Dale Stahlecker.

Sandhill Cranes in Flight

October comes to Colorado's San Luis Valley in many forms. In the surrounding Rio Grande National Forest the aspen trees are ablaze in a golden mist. The most majestic of Colorado's antlered game, the wapiti or elk, are rutting—bugling, fighting for harems, and creating a new generation which will be born the following spring.

In the 7,500-foot-high valley, the fields have turned brown. The last bales of alfalfa dry in the warm sun before being bucked onto flatbeds and hauled to some sheep barn or dairy. The pale barley straw marks the passing of another summer, and field mice scurry about gorging on the nuggets of grain which have not been trucked to storage bins.

The valley is celebrating the end of summer. There is no longing to return to the heat and labor of the passing season. There is no great anticipation of the hardship and bitter cold of the coming winter. There is only fall, the season of harvest in the small agricultural communities that are scattered throughout the valley.

Overhead there is a joyous trumpeting and clacking which causes farmers and field hands to look up from the potato fields. Circling high above, cranes add music to the activities on the ground. There is one group of 40 sandhills floating down from a thermal, and another group of 80 or 100 flapping hard to gain some elevation. They are noisy and hard to ignore. They give the workers below a brief respite from their labor before finding a wind to their liking and filing off toward the Rio Grande in a loose V-formation. The cranes have returned to the San Luis Valley.

Migration. It is one of the wonders of the natural world. It has inspired man—prehistoric hunter, farmer, scientist, and artist—for many thousands of years. In a world which seems to be changing every day, the changing of the seasons and the migration of birds remain unaltered from what they were many centuries ago.

The San Luis Valley is like the neck of an hourglass. It is a constriction through which pass not grains of sand but some 22,000 sandhill and 30 whooping cranes each fall. Although the birds are widespread both during their spring and summer breeding season in the north and their wintering season in the south, they are concentrated in this large intermountain valley during migration.

The valley provides ample food and cover for the cranes during mild fall weather, but it can be a cold, unforgiving place in the winter. During the millennia the cranes have sojourned in the San Luis Valley they have learned, and perhaps passed on genetically, that this is no place for them at that time of the year.

But it is a delightful place for a crane during the fall. The birds begin arriving in the valley in September, and some linger until late November. Monte Vista National Wildlife Refuge attracts major concentrations, as does the Rio Grande—the river that many of the birds will remain near throughout the winter. They feed twice daily in the grain fields and pastures, loaf at midday, and roost for the night in shallow sloughs, marshes, and ponds.

By mid-October the cranes begin to feel the urge to continue their southward migration. The nights are growing colder, and the cranes know that winter is approaching.

The birds move from the roost to the fields to feed early each morning. About 10 o'clock groups of 40, 50, or even 100 start to circle and soar up into the sky. They are testing the winds and the thermals, considering whether to head on south. Early in the fall most groups return to the ground, but they continue to test the air and weigh the decision each morning. As October fades into November more and more cranes leave the valley, flying south, clacking and trumpeting, their sights set on New Mexico's fields and marshes.

It is not unusual to see the migrating cranes in a flapping, calling swirl which gives an impression of confusion. One might believe the birds are lost, but nothing could be further from the truth. They follow the same routes year after year. Some cranes caught in New Mexico in 1960 and marked with neck collars were still alive and migrating 25 years later. Though most birds are not this old, they undoubtedly know their routes as well as human commuters know theirs.

Cranes are cumbersome flyers. They prefer to migrate during daylight hours, when the thermals created by the midday sun provide rising air currents which the cranes ride to gain elevation before gliding down to the next thermal. It is this thermal riding which many observers mistake for being lost or confused.

The spiral is actually more organized than it might at first appear to be. When a flock reaches a thermal there are a few moments of considerable flapping and calling as the birds change direction and start to soar upward. As the cranes circle up in tight flocks, all the birds soar in the same direction. In this formation, there is much less likelihood of a collision than if they were soaring indiscriminately in both directions. When the cranes leave the spiral there are again a few moments of disarray before a V or line takes shape.

Why cranes fly in Vs or lines is not known. The V-formation is probably aerodynamically more efficient, because leading birds "break trail" and lift may be created by the wind crossing the wings of adjacent birds. Presumably a different crane takes the lead each time the flock leaves a thermal, since this is the position requiring the greatest expenditure of energy. The formation may maintain flock unity and the spacing between individuals may keep them from colliding. The birds are also able to see adjacent birds while still having a clear view to the front.

The advantage of this spiraling and gliding form of flight which occurs only during migration is energy conservation. Large birds expend nearly four times as much energy in active flight as they do in passive soaring. To migrate several hundred miles in one day requires considerable amounts of energy. Cranes prepare for their long migrations by building up their fat reserves. However, every means of conserving energy is important to the survival of the birds, and through thousands of years of evolution cranes have developed this passive method of flight as a means of most efficiently making these long journeys.

Cranes also take advantage of winds blowing the direction they wish to travel. In fact, they seek them out, sometimes choosing to fly on blustery days because the winds greatly increase their speed. Spiraling and gliding, while energy efficient, are not time efficient. Much time is spent circling over one spot and progress is slowed. On days with light winds or headwinds, cranes travel at 10 to 35 miles an hour. With a strong tailwind the big birds are sometimes pushed along at the rate of 40 or 50 miles an hour.

Though sandhill and whooping cranes prefer to migrate with the "minimum-effort" technique, migration is actually a combination of flight types. Steady flapping is more common during the morning and evening, or on cloudy days when there is less lift in the air. Cranes also flap intermittently while circling or gliding.

American Kestrel

Migrating flocks are not distinct units. When many cranes are migrating in close proximity, flocks tend to break up and recombine. Individuals or small groups drop back or catch up with new flocks. Reorganization most often occurs when several flocks are spiraling and milling in the same place. Flocks also appear to follow the lead of those ahead, angling for thermals where other flocks are spiraling.

Cranes sometimes migrate as high as 5,000 feet above the ground, but generally less than half that high. They fly highest during the afternoon when there is the greatest amount of lift in the air. Morning and evening flocks tend to be much closer to the ground.

At one time it was thought cranes migrated at night. However, recent studies have shown that they seldom continue to fly after dark. They usually begin a day's flight between 9 and 11 a.m., after the sun has warmed the earth's surface enough to create thermals. Night travel, though uncommon, sometimes occurs when moderate to strong tailwinds are pushing the cranes along. Cranes are also more likely to fly into the night if they are approaching an important destination, a place where they will stay for weeks or months. Generally, though, cranes end migration between two hours before and one-quarter hour after sunset. By then the thermals have disappeared and flying conditions have deteriorated.

All North American cranes migrate considerable distances between their breeding grounds and wintering areas. They utilize a variety of temporary sites while moving between these critical regions. These temporary sites fall into three main categories. "Staging Areas" are those places near the breeding grounds where cranes gather before starting fall migrations. "Traditional Stopovers" are areas where the birds stay for several weeks before completing their journeys. The San Luis Valley is one of these. Migration is temporarily halted while the cranes are in these areas.

Finally, there are "Nontraditional Stopovers," places that are used only overnight while the cranes migrate. This is not to say that some nontraditional stopovers are not regularly used. It means, rather, that the use of the site is of short duration, usually only for one night by a particular flock.

There are many populations of cranes found throughout North America, but those that stop in the San Luis Valley are the greater sandhill cranes of the Rocky Mountains. These birds, some 22,000 of them, are a subspecies of sandhill crane. They are hatched and reared in the mountain valleys of Idaho, western Wyoming, southwestern Montana, northern Utah and northwestern Colorado. They migrate through western Colorado and northern New Mexico to winter in central and southwestern New Mexico, southeastern Arizona and in northern Mexico.

Another population of greater sandhill cranes is found in the Great Lakes states, and those 15,000 birds winter in Florida. There they intermingle with the Florida subspecies which does not migrate at all. There are also two smaller populations of greater sandhill cranes: one group nests in northern Nevada, the other in Oregon and

Washington. The 1,000 or so Nevada birds winter on the lower Colorado River in southern Arizona and the 3,000-plus Oregon and Washington cranes migrate to the Central Valley of California.

As the word "greater" in the name implies, there are smaller forms, or subspecies, of sandhill cranes found in North America. In fact, there are five other subspecies: the lesser, the Canadian, the Mississippi, the Florida, and the Cuban sandhill cranes. The latter three do not migrate, but remain year-round in the states and country for which they are named. They are slightly smaller than the greater sandhills, but larger than the other two migratory forms. Greater sandhill cranes stand four feet tall, weigh about nine to thirteen pounds, and have a wingspan of about six feet or more. Lesser sandhill cranes weigh 40 percent less, are about nine inches shorter, and have a proportionally shorter wingspan. The Canadian subspecies is intermediate in size between the greater and the lesser.

About 20,000 lesser sandhill cranes that breed in southern Alaska migrate down the Pacific Coast, bound for California's Central Valley. Most of the lesser and all of the Canadian sandhills pour south from as far away as Siberia to winter in Texas, New Mexico, and Mexico. Half a million of them migrate over the prairies of Canada and the central United States each fall. Also passing over the prairies are 100 or so whooping cranes. These spectacular white birds fly some 2,400 miles from their breeding grounds in Canada to spend the winter in the coastal marshes of the Aransas National Wildlife Refuge on the Texas coast.

Whooping cranes attain the largest stature of all cranes, though a large male greater sandhill is about the same size as a small female "whooper." Reaching nearly five feet in height, large male whoopers are the tallest birds in North America. They weigh about eleven to sixteen pounds, and have a wingspan approaching seven and a half feet. These snow-white birds have black wing tips and a red crown. They contrast vividly with the subdued gray plumage of the sandhill cranes.

Whooping cranes are also present in the Rocky Mountains, intermingled with the greater sandhill cranes. These large white birds are protected as an endangered species by federal law.

Greater Sandhill Crane

The whoopers that winter in New Mexico are an experimental flock being fostered by both sandhill cranes and humans. There is some evidence that a whooping crane population existed in the Rocky Mountains in the 1800s and persisted into the early 20th century. Yellowstone National Park and surrounding areas in Idaho, Montana, and Wyoming may have been a summering and breeding area. This historic information gave credence to an effort to establish a western whooping crane flock in the same area. Whether this experiment will result in a self-sustaining population is still unknown.

These big white cranes are seen in the San Luis Valley in the fall, arriving with the migrating sandhills. As both species filter down into New Mexico, the whooping cranes become objects of an intense search by a growing number of crane watchers.

Although cranes are usually found close to water when they are on the ground, during migration they do not ordinarily follow water-courses. Instead they head off cross-country directly toward their destinations. When the birds leave the marshes and fields of Colorado, they leave the Rio Grande—which goes east before turning south—and their journey continues over the pinon flats and sagebrush mesas of northern New Mexico. Much of the time they remain unobserved, for human habitations are few and far between. Farther south they travel over the mesas to the west of the Rio Grande. On one of these fingerlike projections of the Pajarito Plateau stands the town of White Rock, a prime spot for watching migrating cranes.

White Rock is perched high above the Rio Grande, and the cranes are usually within 1,000 feet of the ground as they pass overhead. The raucous calling of the milling flocks draws people from their homes. White Rock is 140 miles south of the San Luis Valley crane marshes. The majority of the cranes go by in the early afternoon, provided they have a tailwind. Without one, they'll arrive late in the day.

As the birds continue south, they veer slightly west and fly over Bandelier National Monument and Cochiti Reservoir on the Rio Grande. If they got an early start or are being pushed by a good breeze, they reach Albuquerque by later afternoon. They are often high above this city and its 500,000 residents, however, and the din of civilization drowns out their cries.

The cranes generally fly west of the Rio Grande as they pass over Albuquerque. If there is a strong westerly wind, it pushes them over the eastern part of the city. As they fly southeast they cross over Albuquerque International Airport. Air traffic controllers occasionally see clouds of birds on their radar screens and must warn pilots of the potential danger. Fortunately, no collisions between the cranes and airplanes over Albuquerque have been reported. But elsewhere in the United States collisions have damaged aircraft and killed cranes, including at least one whooping crane.

Once they pass over New Mexico's largest city, the cranes have officially reached their winter home. The weary birds seek out familiar haunts, heading for sandbar roosts on the Rio Grande or nearby fields to feed. Earlier arrivals welcome the new birds. The "all-clear" call rises in unison from the fields and river roosts as the migrants circle down to join their kin.

For some cranes the journey is over. They will go no farther. Others travel on south for another 75 miles to the Bosque del Apache National Wildlife Refuge near San Antonio, New Mexico. Some continue on into Mexico before the urge to travel wanes.

Cranes that leave the San Luis Valley early in the day or are pushed by tailwinds make the trip to the wintering grounds in one day. Most birds are able to do this. But several times each fall a series of events occurs which can result in a large number of cranes failing to complete the journey in one day.

The cranes in the San Luis Valley can feel the declining air pressure that precedes a cold front from the Pacific Northwest. This agitates them: it forebodes snow, cold and clouds which might trap them, even for a short time, in the valley. The warm, sunny weather south of the front also gives them good thermals for spiraling, and many anxious cranes are soon on their way.

However, an approaching weather system also involves a condition that can be detrimental to the birds' migration. Since most North American cold fronts move from northwest to southeast, winds ahead of these fronts blow mostly from the southwest. These winds, though usually light, blow partially or directly into the faces of the oncoming cranes, slowing their progress. The result is a reduced flight distance; cranes that could have made the 210-mile journey to the wintering grounds in a single day may travel only 165 miles or less.

The cranes which encounter these conditions are forced to use a nontraditional stopover on the lower Jemez River 40 miles south of White Rock. Some cranes do not even make it that far. Each year some cranes stop overnight on the dry mesa tops between White Rock and the Jemez River. These birds of marshes and fields look out of place among the scattered pinon and juniper trees. But the following morning they are again on their way and soon are on the wintering grounds.

One thing is certain. Each fall 22,000 cranes pass through northern New Mexico on their annual journey. They leave many excited and enchanted people in their wake. These are the things that move us to seek out the cranes—their constant chatter, crane flocks against a brilliant sunset, the magic of their migration itself—and a glimpse perhaps of a magnificent white crane.

A brisk wind sweeps across the deck of the tour boat. It is cold and the people by the rails adjust their collars and huddle a little closer, trying to get warm. The wise tourists are crowded inside the small cabin. Laughing gulls follow the boat, pasted against a dark, cloudy sky. Herons and shorebirds flit past the vessel, but hands stay in pockets and binoculars inside of coats. It is foul weather for bird watching.

"There's a family of whooping cranes up ahead on the left," crackles the captain's voice over the loudspeakers of the *M. V. Whooping Crane.* Binoculars materialize and the cabin empties. The people crowd forward to catch a glimpse of the birds they have traveled so far to see. The cold is forgotten, and delighted smiles appear under a sea of binoculars, all pointed toward two large white birds and their rusty offspring.

The boat edges closer while the cranes continue to forage in the tidal marsh, unconcerned by the boatload of people staring at them. After a few minutes one of the adults captures a blue crab, struggles with it briefly, then swallows it whole. It is a good half hour before the wind dulls the crane watchers' appetites and they begin to filter back into the cabin.

Aransas National Wildlife Refuge in Texas has long been the winter home of the whooping cranes. Until relatively recently, 11 years ago in fact, it was the only *sure* place where one could see these majestic, rare birds in the wild. Each winter thousands of people come from all over the United States—and the world—to see them. And the best way to see them is from a tour boat.

Information about whooping cranes before the 1930s is scant. It is known that they nested in what is now Louisiana and from Iowa up through the prairies of central Canada. Whoopers may also have bred farther north in Canada, farther west along the Texas coast, and as far west as the northern Rockies. Cranes from northern breeding grounds migrated to the Texas and Louisiana coasts for the winter. Some birds wintered in the Texas and Mexico highlands, intermingling with sandhill cranes which were abundant there. Whoopers migrated across the Appalachians and wintered along the Atlantic Coast as late as the 1830s. There may have been nonmigratory resident whooping cranes in Florida, Alabama, and Georgia.

Even then whooping cranes were probably not abundant. Estimates of the numbers of whooping cranes around the 1870s range from 700 to 1,300.

But as the marshlands were lost to the plow with the advent of farming on the prairies, whooping crane numbers plummeted. By the 1930s, only the birds wintering at Aransas and a small resident flock of 10 to 15 cranes in Louisiana remained. The nonmigratory Louisiana birds were decimated by a hurricane in 1940, although a few survived. The last Louisiana crane was taken into captivity in 1949, leaving only the Aransas flock to perpetuate the species.

Whooping Cranes at Aransas National Wildlife Refuge

For years, little was known about the Aransas whooping cranes. The last recorded nesting attempt in the Canadian prairie occurred in 1922. Though a few pairs of cranes returned to Aransas each fall with new young at their sides, their nesting grounds were unknown. The few remaining birds left Aransas in the spring, were irregularly sighted in migration at such places as the Platte River in Nebraska, but then disappeared into the Canadian northlands.

The number of birds continued to slide. Wildlife officials and crane lovers could only helplessly wait to see how many would return to Aransas each fall. The designation of Aransas National Wildlife Refuge in 1937 protected the wintering grounds, but at first it did little to stop the decline. By 1941, only 13 adults and two juveniles appeared at Aransas.

At the end of World War II, the National Audubon Society and the U.S. Fish and Wildlife Service began an intensive study of the whooping crane. For the next decade, Audubon's Robert Porter Allen gathered a base of information on the wintering habits of the whoopers at Aransas and searched for their breeding grounds in Canada. He made repeated trips to the sub-Arctic in the late 1940s and early 1950s, but all met with failure. The whooping cranes seemed to vanish at the northern edge of the Canadian prairies.

Finally, late in the summer of 1954, a firefighter flying over Wood Buffalo National Park in northwestern Canada saw whooping cranes below. In 1955 Allen located several pair with young—the 33-year-old mystery had been solved. At last the whooping cranes could be monitored and managed on both their breeding and wintering grounds. The whooping cranes began a gradual climb back, and today more than 100 of them return to Aransas each November.

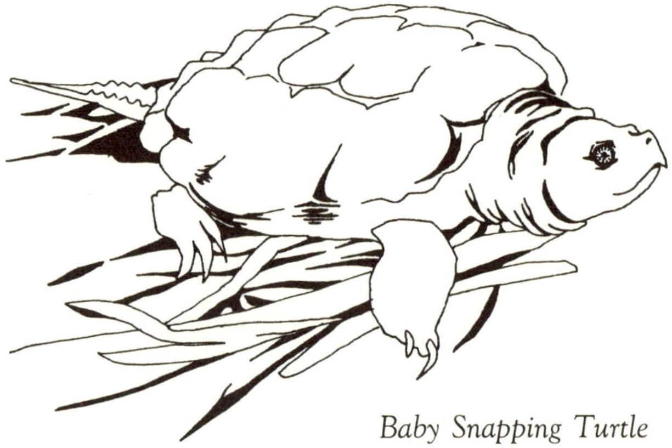

Baby Snapping Turtle

It was logical that these birds migrated along a more-or-less straight course from Wood Buffalo to Aransas. Indeed, sightings of the whooping cranes over the years were along this direct-line route. Because there were so few birds, it was difficult to piece together their exact migration route. It required the development of a new technology to finally document the route taken by the great white birds.

In the early 1980s, flightless young whoopers were captured in late summer at Wood Buffalo National Park by Canadian and American research biologists. A small radio transmitter was attached to one leg of some of the young cranes. The signals from the transmitters enabled teams of biologists to follow families of cranes and to locate them at night.

Five different cranes were tracked from Wood Buffalo to Aransas. All left between late September and early October. They arrived at Aransas in mid-November. On the average the trip took 29 days, 20 in Canada and nine in the United States. The Canadian portion of the journey is 900 miles, the U.S. portion is 1,500. However, many whooping cranes spent up to two weeks feeding in Canadian grain fields, building up fat reserves for the flight to Texas. While actually migrating, the cranes usually traveled several hundred miles a day. One family flew 1,140 miles, from South Dakota to Aransas, in just two days.

Aransas National Wildlife Refuge contains 54,000 acres, but the whooping cranes limit most of their activities to the coastal marshes. Within a few days after arrival, each adult pair or family

Sandhill Crane and Mule Deer

group stakes out a territory that will be theirs throughout the winter. The territories average 286 acres in size, and though some overlapping use occurs, the bulk of each territory is used only by its occupants. The male is very aggressive in defending his area.

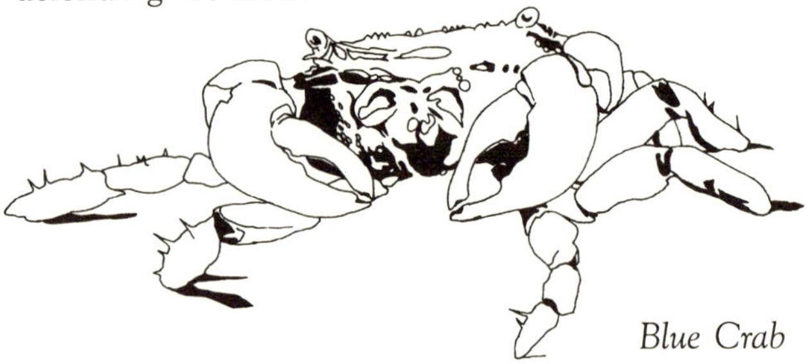

Blue Crab

Most pairs of whooping cranes raise only one chick. It will spend its first winter with its parents in Aransas. It stays close to the female, and when she captures prey the young bird gives a soft, begging call. About half of what the female captures she will give to her chick. The male will also feed the chick, or colt, but often forages several hundred yards from his offspring and mate.

The Aransas whooping cranes feed mostly on aquatic animals. Blue crabs and several types of clams are the preferred and most important foods. Fiddler crabs, shrimp, eels, snakes, and crayfish are also eaten. Acorns, wolfberries, and other types of vegetation complete the diet.

Whooping cranes pair for life, which may be 20 years or longer in the wild. It is believed that this lifelong bond is important to the birds because of the extended period, 8 to 11 months, that the young remain with the adults. After such a long rearing period, there would be too little time to establish a new pair bond before the next nesting season.

Although almost all pairs of whooping cranes which arrive at Aransas bring only one chick with them, most lay two eggs in their Wood Buffalo nests. This led biologists to conclude that the second egg was, in most cases, being wasted. In the late 1960s, these "spare" eggs were removed from the nests and hatched at the Patuxent Wildlife Research Center, a facility in Maryland operated by the U.S. Fish and Wildlife Service.

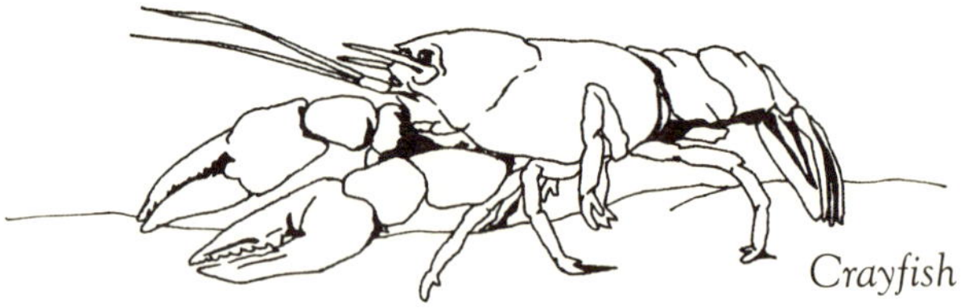

Crayfish

The practice has continued and a captive flock of about 40 whooping cranes is maintained there.

In 1975 a more ambitious experiment was begun. The spare eggs were taken to Grays Lake National Wildlife Refuge in southeastern Idaho. There they were hatched by greater sandhill cranes, replacing the eggs the sandhills had laid. Once the whooping crane eggs hatch, the sandhill cranes rear the young as they would their own chicks. And so began a second flock of whooping cranes, the flock which winters in New Mexico.

Dr. Rod Drewien of the Idaho Cooperative

Wildlife Research Unit has been working with the foster parent project since its beginning. He and Ernie Kuyt of the Canadian Wildlife Service collect the eggs in Wood Buffalo National Park and place them in the sandhill crane nests in Idaho the next day. Drewien and his assistants monitor the rearing and growth of the young whoopers, their migration to the San Luis Valley, and finally their trips with their foster parents to the New Mexican wintering grounds.

The sandhills chosen for the project were selected because of their propensity for wintering on Bosque del Apache National Wildlife Refuge. The biologists felt the chicks could be better protected at the refuge than if they wintered elsewhere. However, the whoopers soon proved to have minds of their own and now winter throughout the middle Rio Grande Valley.

Slowly over the last 11 years the experimental flock has grown. Their number exceeded 10 in 1978 and 20 in 1983. Between 1983 and 1985, at least 29 whooping cranes have spent each winter in New Mexico.

These Rocky Mountain whooping cranes have learned much from their sandhill foster parents. And, as one might expect, their habits are somewhat different from the white birds which winter at Aransas. Where the Aransas birds feed mostly on small aquatic animals, more than 90 percent of the winter diet of the foster flock is corn and other waste grains found in fields. Much of the time they feed at Bosque del Apache and at Belen and Bernardo State refuges, where corn is planted especially for geese and cranes.

The young foster whooping cranes, like other young cranes, remain with their parents through-

Immature Bald Eagle with Snow Goose

out their first winter. Pairs of sandhills do not set up winter territories. Instead, large flocks of sandhills roost at night in shallow marshes near the Rio Grande, and then leave at dawn to feed in fields. Most remain there all day, but they return to the marshes again as light fades. The young foster whooping cranes do as their parents, and they continue this pattern as they mature to subadults and adults.

The cranes share their winter home at Bosque del Apache with thousands of snow geese. These beautiful birds, which are also white with black wing tips like the whooping cranes, breed in the Arctic tundra of Canada, and to a lesser degree in Siberia and Alaska. They migrate down the Rocky Mountains each fall, also arriving at the Bosque refuge in large numbers in mid-November.

The refuge is also home to thousands of wintering mallards and other ducks. Mule deer feed in the corn fields and coyotes lope along the edges of feeding flocks of geese and other birds, looking for crippled or sick geese or cranes. Bald eagles are also drawn to the refuge by the abundance of waterfowl. They, too, prey on sick and wounded birds.

Like Aransas, where 64,000 visitors were counted in 1985, the Bosque refuge is also a big attraction. An estimated 80,000 people came to view wildlife during 1985, and most came during the winter months when the cranes and geese were abundant. Their massive morning and evening flights excite all who visit the refuge. And although all of the animals make the trip worthwhile, it is the sight of one or more whooping cranes which provides the icing on an

Coyote

already rich cake. They are majestic, towering over their smaller sandhill cousins and foster parents.

The Rocky Mountain whooping cranes have not yet mated and produced young, and some biologists believe what happens to the birds during their winter visits to New Mexico directly affects what the birds do during the spring nesting season. Information from recent studies of pair bonding among whooping cranes at Aransas may be helpful in the management of the New Mexico population.

Pairing by whooping cranes in the Aransas flock is a long process, and begins on the wintering grounds when the birds are young. Pair formation is difficult to study, because all whoopers older than yearlings look so much alike. Since 1977, most chicks have been captured and marked with colored leg bands before they leave Wood Buffalo National Park. With more and more birds marked, individuals can be recognized and their social development followed. Subadult whoopers, those which have molted into adult plumage but have not paired or nested, stay together in flocks at Aransas. They do not set up territories. These nonbreeders may be found in areas between defended territories of the adults, and frequently near the territory where they spent their first winter with their parents. Subadult flocks also move about more than territorial adults, and several flocks may come together to take advantage of unusual food concentrations.

Marked birds which have eventually paired have been observed together as subadults for at least one and often several winters. They stay closer to each other than to other cranes. Pairs which have eventually raised young have also been seen migrating and spending the summer together, even though still too young to nest. Whooping cranes become sexually mature between the ages of four and six.

The bond between a pair of adult cranes is maintained by ritualized posturing and vocalizations known as "unison calling." The birds also dance, male and female facing one another, leaping and bowing gracefully with outspread wings. Solo dancing by the male occurs in early winter, but as spring approaches dancing by the pair increases. Dancing by adult pairs appears to be more common in spring migration and probably is most frequent on the nesting grounds.

Until recently it was impossible to identify adult pairs. Circumstantial evidence indicated that each pair returned to the same winter territory each year, but this could not be proven because all the birds were very similar in appearance. But the marking program has made it possible to recognize individuals. In about half the adult pairs, one or both members are now marked. Resightings of these marked birds have proven that they do indeed return to the same wintering sites each year.

New pairs usually attempt to establish a winter territory near the one where the male spent his first winter. This strong homing to the old wintering territory appears to be the reason that the area used by whooping cranes at Aransas has not increased much since 1951, although the population has tripled since then.

Black Skimmers

Whooping cranes use only 37 percent of the suitable coastal marhsland at or near Aransas. Instead of moving into an unoccupied area, the new pairs try to carve out a territory near where the male was raised. For example, there were seven territories averaging 400 acres on the east shore of Aransas during the winter of 1950–51. In 1971–72 there were 10 territories in the same area, but there was enough marsh there that the average remained at 400 acres. By 1984–85, however, there were 16 territories and the average size had decreased to 286 acres.

Although it has been rare for the whooping cranes to pioneer new territories, it would appear the birds will need to soon. Saturation of some portions of the winter range appears to have been reached. Several pairs that have nested in Wood Buffalo in recent years have failed to acquire a territory the following winter at Aransas.

Some pioneering by cranes into areas adjacent to the Aransas refuge has occurred. It is impossible to predict how high crane densities will become in the future, but a range expansion may be necessary if the population continues to increase. From the low of 15 in 1941, the flock has increased to 97 in 1985, and as many as 115 whooping cranes may winter at Aransas in 1986. In the 1986 breeding season alone, 20 young whooping cranes reached fledging age, the age at which they took their first flight. For the tall young whooping cranes, the wings and feathers become strong enough to sustain flight when they are 75–90 days old.

But all this could be lost in one swift blow. A hurricane, like the one that wiped out the Louisiana birds in the 1940s, could hit the Aransas coastal marshes and again seriously reduce the size of the flock. An oil or toxic chemical spill could have devastating effects.

That's what makes the Rocky Mountain whooping cranes so important to the overall survival of the species. All the eggs are not in one basket if there are two or more flocks of whooping cranes in North America.

Snow Geese

Throughout their winter range sandhill cranes are getting edgy by early February. We humans generally do not consider February to be part of spring, but sandhill cranes have a much different perspective on life. By mid-February, the cranes feel it's high time to head back north.

Robins are supposed to be the first birds of spring, but sandhills certainly do their share to bring spring north with them. Geese and some ducks may get an earlier start, and bald and golden eagles are not far behind, but these relatively silent migrants don't get nearly as much attention as a musical ensemble of cranes.

The majority of sandhills will have left the wintering areas before March, regardless of the weather. March arrives, whether as a lion or a lamb, to find the cranes north of their winter homes, and many a time a "lion" blizzard has made life rough for these early migrants as they head toward a northland still held in winter's icy grip.

There is, however, a reason for this early departure. After this early journey, all sandhill cranes stop part way to their breeding grounds to rest and socialize. They will remain at a spring stopover for four to six weeks, gathering strength for the next leg of the trip and strengthening pair bonds. The paired cranes dance together in meadows and fields, they feed on corn they passed over during their fall migration and build up fat reserves for the final flight to the nesting grounds.

The Rocky Mountain sandhill cranes stop again in the San Luis Valley. The lesser sandhills that wintered on the plains of eastern New Mexico and Texas use the Platte River in Nebraska for their spring stopover. They make an impressive sight, as some 500,000 birds leave roosts at morning to mill around the farms of this Plains state. The whooping cranes of Aransas remain on the wintering grounds the longest. Most do not leave Texas until the first week in April, but they may stay only a short time on the Platte if they stop at all. Many of the Aransas whoopers simply hurry on north to their nesting territories at Wood Buffalo National Park.

The whooping cranes of the Rocky Mountains however, do not remain in New Mexico until April. If they have inherited a preference for staying longer on the wintering grounds, they nevertheless seem to get caught up in the excitement and frenzy of thousands of greater sandhills eager for their journey back north. The great white birds leave New Mexico in late February with the sandhills.

The northern migration starts very much like the trip south. The birds begin their midmorning ritual of spiraling up into the sky, testing their wings, the thermals, and the breezes. High above the Rio Grande they ply the air, circling and calling. Many of the birds leave the Bosque refuge and move 50 to 75 miles farther north. Just that short flight reduces the length of the trip required back to the San Luis Valley.

Finally, *the* morning has arrived, and with a great deal of noise the flocks break out of the top of their spiral and head north to Colorado. For the first few days the numbers are small—perhaps only 200, 500, or 1,000 cranes will make the move. But then a mass exodus begins: 3,000 to 4,000 cranes depart each day. At that rate, only five or six days of steady northward migration is needed for most of the cranes to leave the fields and sandbars of the Rio Grande Valley. Some cranes remain in New Mexico for a few more weeks, but usually once the birds really start leaving, 70 to 80 percent will make the move in a week or less.

The route of the Rocky Mountain cranes is practically the same one used in fall. Massive flights of thousands of cranes are spotted 500 to 1,000 feet overhead as they fly over Albuquerque. They are bunched early in the day and the flights are typically spectacular, and noisy.

Cranes depart the fields between 9:00 and 11:00 A.M. It takes only an hour for the large flocks to reach the big city, and wave after wave flies over, drawing a lot of attention. People congregate at office windows downtown to watch the birds fly by. Occasionally, the white body and black wing tip of a whooping crane stand out in a V-formation of gray cranes.

In the streets of Albuquerque's Old Town or in its North Valley yards, people stop their work to stare at the birds. The crescendo of crane noise sometimes even exceeds that of traffic.

As quickly as it started, it ends. A straggling flock or two hurries by, but the masses have moved north. Beyond Albuquerque, there are fewer humans to note the birds' passing until they again reach White Rock. Few people see the birds rise the thermals coming off the dark volcanic rock of Cochiti Dam's south face. This man-made solar collector gives the birds a big boost high into the sky.

Sandhill Crane Roost on the Platte River

Ninety percent of the cranes pass over White Rock between noon and 3:00 P.M. People stop eating lunch to rush outside and watch the circling cranes. Children in playgrounds search the azure sky until one of them spots the birds and points them out to his playmates. Friends call each other and the message is something like, "Quick, go outside. The cranes are coming and there's *millions* of them!"

A continuous succession of V-formations arrive, spiral in the thermals over the town, and then move on north. Again the change is abrupt. One moment the sky is full of calling birds, then it's empty. The calls of the cranes fade off in the distance, leaving only memories of the massive passage of birds that has just taken place.

Much of the migration again occurs to the west of the Rio Grande. At the north end of the Espanola Valley, 20 miles from White Rock, a large mesa rises some 1,000 feet above the valley floor. Its black basalt slopes produce some tremendous thermals. Like surfers who can't ignore a good wave, the cranes angle toward the mesa. This natural elevator gives them a big boost before they strike out over the pinon- and sagebrush-covered highlands of northern New Mexico. It is mid-afternoon, two-thirds of their journey is behind them, but the southern edge of the San Luis Valley is still 80 miles away.

In the fall the birds can count on the Rio Grande and Jemez roosts if they cannot complete the final third of the journey to the wintering grounds in a single day. In spring they face nothing but sage and trees from here to the San Luis Valley. Although they can stop in the open or fly at night if necessary, they much prefer to reach the valley before the sun sets on this portion of their trip. The Rio Grande can no longer be used because, although it is only a short distance to the east, it is now hundreds of feet below the plateau in a long, deep canyon. It may be fine for rafting and fishing, but it's of little value to migrating cranes.

Most cranes make the trip without having to stop overnight. As in fall, weather is a big factor. Frontal systems from the northwest still dominate the weather picture, but southwest breezes which slow fall migration now work to the cranes' benefit, propelling the birds toward Colorado. In order to use these favorable winds though, the cranes must fly toward storms rather than in front of them. At times they have to skirt approaching snow squalls as they fly north, and sometimes they disappear into a wall of light snow. But the winds behind them push them on, and ordinarily they complete the trip before dark.

Storms can pose a problem even after they have passed. On February 23, 1985, a major snowstorm dropped six inches of snow on the New Mexico highlands and rain fell in the Rio Grande Valley. No cranes could leave during the storm. The 24th dawned clear and bright, and 3,000 cranes caught the midmorning thermals along the river and headed north. No southwest wind pushed them along, so progress was slower than usual.

Still all went well until they reached the mesas near White Rock in midafternoon. Here the snow was reflecting the sunlight, and the ground had not been heated enough to create thermals. That

Killdeer

made travel difficult at best, and the birds had to resort to more energy-consuming flapping flight instead of the usual thermal-riding and gliding. Although almost all the birds passed beyond the Espanola Valley that day, many probably did not make it to the San Luis Valley and had to spend the night on the chaparral highlands of northern New Mexico. About 500 unfortunate cranes were seen near the small town of Tres Piedras on the morning of the 25th, and many more were probably scattered along the route to Colorado. With clear skies on the 25th, however, they completed their journey to the marshes of the San Luis Valley without further difficulty.

By the end of the first week in March few cranes are left in New Mexico. Only scattered flocks of cranes which have wintered farther south move through after that. During all of March and into early April the cranes make the San Luis Valley their home. They rest and feed, storing energy needed for the first month on the nesting grounds where food may be scarce early in the season.

Not all of the cranes stay that long. It appears that several thousand lesser sandhill cranes move up the Rio Grande with their Rocky Mountain relatives. For example, 26,000 cranes were counted at White Rock during the 1985 spring migration, although there are only an estimated 22,000 greater sandhills in the Rocky Mountain flock. No doubt some of the lesser sandhills had joined them for this leg of the northward journey.

One would think the lesser sandhills would have flown around the southern tip of the Rocky Mountains and then up the plains to the Platte Valley in Nebraska. It appears that these lesser sandhills get caught up in the migration frenzy of their greater sandhill companions and get swept along off their normal course. Undoubtedly these birds move east toward the Platte Valley after a short stopover. They leave the San Luis Valley over a pass in the Sangre de Cristo Mountains, and then angle northeast across the Colorado plains.

The Big Bend portion of the Platte, between Overton and Grand Island, Nebraska, is a mecca for migrating waterfowl. In late February and early March, there are tens of thousands of mallards, pintails, Canada and white-fronted geese. Snow geese arrive in the thousands, although they are even more abundant along the Missouri River several hundred miles to the east. These same snows and white-fronts wintered along the Gulf Coast of Texas and Louisiana and in the highlands of northern Mexico. A few may even have shared Aransas National Wildlife Refuge with the whooping cranes. But by late March, when the greatest densities of cranes occur, many of the geese and ducks have already left.

Many sandhill cranes stop at the Platte in the fall, though it is usually only an overnight stop on their trip to Texas or New Mexico. But when they leave their winter grounds in the spring, the Platte is their immediate destination. They will stay four to six weeks before continuing on to their breeding grounds in the far north.

Sandhills, like all other cranes, mate for life. With the nesting season approaching, they become more sexually active. Dancing pairs of cranes are often seen in the meadows near the Platte. The

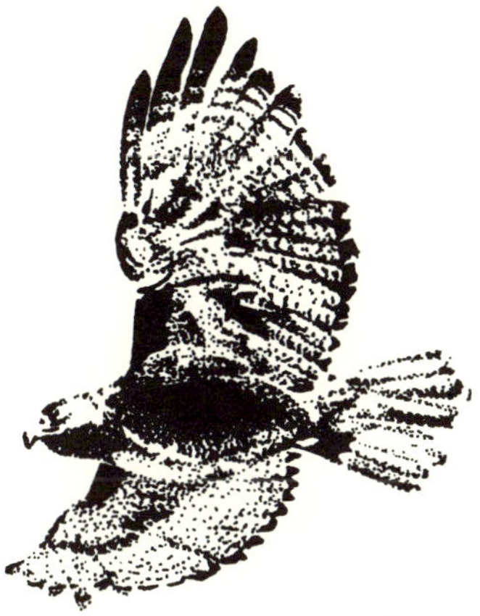

Red-tailed Hawk

male and female face each other and begin by spreading their wings and leaping gracefully into the air. They then bow and leap again. Dances may be short, or they may last for several minutes.

The dance was thought to be a very important part of the pair-bonding process in sandhill cranes. Since more dancing occurs on the Platte than on the wintering grounds, it was also thought that many pairings took place there. It is difficult to study the pair bonds of the lesser sandhill cranes, for they travel several thousand miles each year. It would be almost impossible for biologists to keep track of even one of these cranes long enough to document its pairings and separations.

Detailed studies have, however, been made on Florida sandhill cranes which remain within a much smaller area, usually less than two hundred square miles, as unpaired subadults. Again, marking cranes with colored leg bands made it possible to distinguish individuals so that they could be monitored through several years. Forty-eight cranes were marked and studied for four years. These cranes began to form pairs when 18 to 20 months old. Many of these pairings did not last, for the average subadult Florida sandhill paired five times before successfully breeding. The rearing of young was found to be the most important factor in cementing the lifetime bond in these cranes. Novice pairs that did not produce young were not as likely to stay together as pairs that were successful.

It is likely that the pairing process for the lesser and Canadian sandhill cranes that gather each year on the Platte is similar to that exhibited by their resident Florida relatives. Two dancing subadults may not remain a lifelong pair, but eventually they will find mates with whom they will stay.

The crane colony of the Platte is a spectacular sight. An estimated half-million birds, virtually all the lesser and Canadian sandhill cranes in the world, are concentrated in a relatively small area. They have been stopping here for as long as they have been migrating. Their spring dances are as much a part of this land as the buffalo wallows once were.

Cranes roost on the river each night and then leave in the morning to hunt in nearby meadows for insects, worms, and other small prey. They then move to nearby fields to forage for waste grain from last fall's harvest. Rarely do they range more than three miles from the river's banks. During midday they usually return to the meadows to loaf, but fly to the fields in the afternoon.

A drive along the roads adjacent to the Platte shows winter has not retreated too far north. The trees are bare, the meadows a faded yellow. Cold winds send clouds scuttling across the sky above the cornfields that trail away from the river for mile after mile. The cornstalks have been beaten down by harvesters, cattle, and winter snows, but an occasional rebel stands straight, its ragged leaves fluttering in the breeze.

The cranes are everywhere. Their gray silhouettes are often hard to discern against the dull brown fields, but as you drive closer they walk warily from the roads. Pairs and small flocks fly between fields and meadows. Threesomes and occasional foursomes indicate family groups which have not yet broken up; the young of the previous summer are identifiable because they still lack the reddish cap of the adults. Their voices are finally changing from the high-pitched peepings of youth to the throaty call of the adult. They will soon be forced to leave by their parents who are already preparing for the upcoming nesting attempt, or they may become separated from them in the general confusion of the massive morning and evening roosting flights on the Platte.

These flights are without doubt one of the most impressive bird shows in the world. Having driven through miles of crane-infested cornfields until late afternoon, the visitor should now head for the river. Any of the bridges which cross the Platte between Grand Island and Overton provides good access to the evening show. Better still, one should try to reserve a place in a blind near one of the favored roosts. Viewing blinds are open to the public at both the National Audubon Society's Rowe Sanctuary, near Kearney, and the Platte River Whooping Crane Critical Habitat Trust's Mormon Island Crane Meadows, near Grand Island.

Observers should arrive at the blind about an hour before sunset. The sun is low and a scattering of clouds give promise of a brilliant

sunset as a backdrop for the scene about to be enacted. The river is empty of cranes, though ducks and geese may be present. All is quiet except for the gurgling river quietly shifting the sands of its bed. In most places it is only knee deep. This shallowness makes it an ideal roost for cranes.

The river is quiet, the cranes are not. In the background the wet meadows surrounding the viewing blind are alive in chorus. The birds may be standing patiently, preening themselves, or walking about trying to find one last-minute tidbit before the sun disappears. But they are all talking, calling.

As many as 30,000 cranes have been counted in a single 700-acre meadow before the evening flight. They seem to be waiting for the sun to reach the right position before they begin their dramatic return to the river. It is as if they know that proper lighting is necessary to provide the full effect of their boisterous salute to the end of another day.

The flocks that seem most anxious take wing first. They fly up and down the river, their loud calling giving the impression that they are discussing the attributes of the various sandbars hidden beneath the surface of the water. Finally they find one which satisfies them and they land, gracefully, by heading into the light westerly breeze. Scattered flocks soon dot the river to the next bend, and probably beyond.

The crescendo rises in the nearby meadows, the orchestra building for a resounding finale. A fiery ball creeps ever closer to the western horizon, painting the clouds orange, red, and finally pink.

Cranes depart the meadows in increasing numbers. More and more flocks cruise up and down the river. As the day wanes, they spend less time searching, trusting the choices made by earlier flocks. The river in front of the blind begins to fill with cranes—first hundreds, then thousands. They stand in the shallow water and continue to talk to the birds still searching for a suitable place to spend the night. As darkness creeps across the river the last flocks descend to the sandbars. A mile of river 300 yards wide may hold 25,000 cranes—a veritable sea of sandhills. They will chatter for hours, gradually growing silent as they fall asleep, their bills laid across their shoulders or tucked under their scapular feathers.

The cranes remain in the water all night. They sleep, but lightly and intermittently, waking at intervals, stretching and looking around for predators. In a roost of 25,000 birds, dozens are alert at any given moment.

Occasionally something upsets the sentries, and for a while the birds will call excitedly. Other than that the river roosts are relatively quiet throughout the night. The progressively colder temperature does not seem to disturb the cranes.

The first hint of light growing on the eastern skyline does not go unnoticed by the sandhills on the Platte. They greet it with a wake-up call as the clouds begin to turn pink ahead of the rising sun. The river comes alive again with the noise of the awakening multitude. As soon as it is light enough to see clearly the birds are up and away, seeking out the nearest meadow for breakfast. The roosts empty quickly, and by sunrise most of the birds have left for feeding areas.

The number of cranes along the Platte builds throughout the month of March. They are poised for their invasion of the northlands. They continue to feed, but in late March they resume the ritual of the morning spiral. By early April, when the whooping cranes are leaving Aransas, the sandhill cranes have left the Platte behind. The Canadian sandhills have at least another 800 miles to go before they nest. Many lesser sandhills will fly to the western coast of Alaska, 3,000 miles from the Platte Valley, before their spring migration is complete. Some 70,000 will fly into Russian airspace while crossing the Bering Sea, bound for marshes in eastern Siberia. When they arrive there in late April or early May, they will have traveled nearly 3,400 miles to reach a bleak, cold marshland where they will once again raise young.

For the greater sandhill and whooping cranes in the San Luis Valley, the final leg of the migration is much shorter. Grays Lake National Wildlife Refuge in Idaho is only 475 miles away, and even the most northerly nesting site in western Montana is less than 800. These cranes are also usually northbound by the end of the first week of April.

First they must fly over the Continental Divide, northwest of the San Luis Valley. They must spiral high to cross these mountains with peaks that exceed 14,000 feet. After that, they angle northwest across the mountains and plateaus of western Colorado. How far they get in the first day is determined by how long it takes to cross the Divide and, as always, how early in the day they get started. A marked whooping crane was once observed in the San Luis Valley in the morning and at Ouray National Wildlife Refuge in Utah that evening, a trip of 275 miles. A favored overnight stopping place is the meadows adjacent to Fruitgrowers Reservoir near Delta, Colorado. As many as five foster whooping cranes have been seen at that stopover in a single spring. This is about 150 miles from the San Luis Valley.

From Ouray National Wildlife Refuge on Utah's Green River, the crane's route leads north over the Uintah Mountains. Again the birds must fly over 13,000-foot peaks on their way north. Many sandhill cranes stop for several days in the upper Bear River Valley in southwestern Wyoming, perhaps resting after the high-altitude flight they have just completed. Though Grays Lake, 475 miles from the San Luis Valley, is conceivably a two-day trip under favorable conditions, it appears that most cranes take up to a week to make the journey.

Unpaired sandhill cranes may tarry along the way, not leaving the San Luis Valley until May. The breeding instinct is stronger in older, paired sandhills, and they arrive on the nesting grounds early to reclaim their 20- to 40-acre territories at Grays Lake and elsewhere in Idaho, Wyoming, Montana, Utah and Colorado marshlands.

Meanwhile, many of the whooping cranes are leaving Texas for Canada. Radiotelemetry has helped to provide new information about their annual trip. One yearling reached Wood Buffalo National Park 13 days after departing from Aransas. A pair of two-year-olds traveled much slower. They spent three weeks on the Platte, often dancing together in the meadows.

The pull of the breeding grounds is strong for the adults. One pair with their radio-tagged yearling left Aransas on April 6, 1984. They spent a week in Kansas and arrived in central Saskatchewan on April 26. They abandoned their nearly grown youngster there and apparently continued directly to the nesting grounds. There they built a new nest and laid two eggs, one of which ended up in an Idaho greater sandhill crane nest.

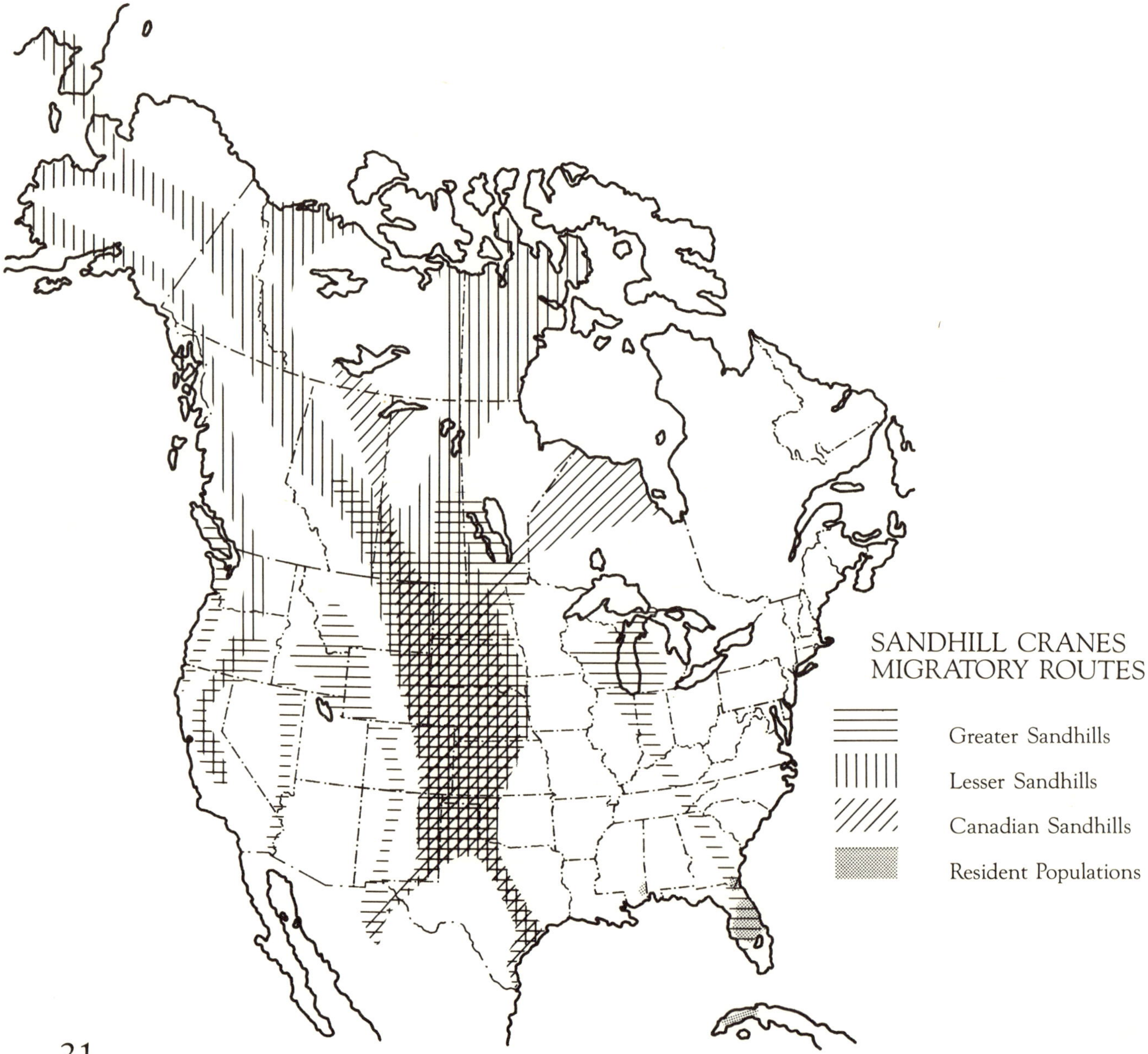
SANDHILL CRANES
MIGRATORY ROUTES
Greater Sandhills
Lesser Sandhills
Canadian Sandhills
Resident Populations

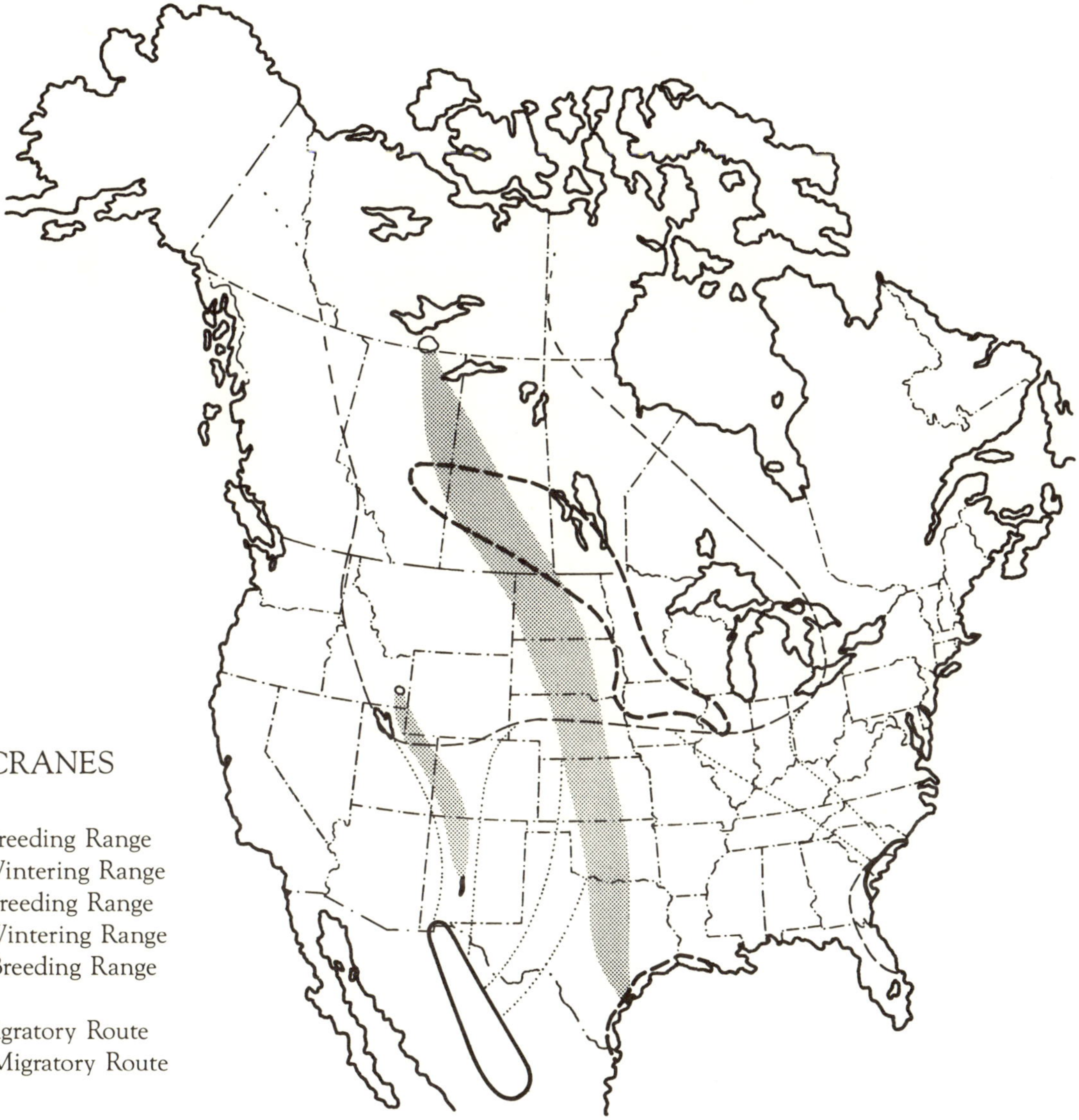

WHOOPING CRANES

Present Breeding Range
Present Wintering Range
Known Breeding Range
Known Wintering Range
Possible Breeding Range

Major Migratory Route
Historic Migratory Route

Based on maps from *Cranes of the World* by P. A. Johnsgaard, Indiana University Press, 1982.

From her nest on the dead cattails, the female greater sandhill crane has a commanding view of the marsh. The open water reflects the clear blue sky above, and only a slight ripple is noticeable from the gentle breeze.

In the distance a creature is approaching. It is making a terrible noise as it streaks across the otherwise still waters, leaving a long, wide trail behind it.

As the object comes closer, the crane rises carefully from her nest and the egg she has been incubating with her mate since late April. He is standing guard nearby, and as the roaring beast comes closer they flee. They are alarmed but not panicky—this thing has come before.

The airboat pulls alongside the nest and one of the men on board reaches down and grabs the egg. It is still warm, and he quickly exchanges it with his companion for a similar egg. The sandhill's egg is placed inside a cushioned box and the engine roars again as the boat speeds away.

After the noise fades into a distant, persistent buzz, the crane returns to her nest. The sight of the egg reassures her and triggers her ancient instincts. We'll never know if she actually notices any difference between this egg and the one she has laid herself, but she covers it, thereby accepting it.

The egg they have placed in the nest had been laid and nurtured by whooping cranes in Wood Buffalo National Park in northern Canada. With just days remaining before it would hatch, the two biologists had moved it from Canada to Idaho. They had flown across the Canadian marshlands in a helicopter a day or two before and landed near the nest. The female whooping crane, like the sandhill, moved back from the approaching machine. She and her mate watched with apprehension as one man waded to the nest and removed one of her eggs.

After the helicopter had flown away, one of the cranes returned to the nest to complete the job they had begun a month earlier.

The egg, along with those taken from other whooping crane nests, was placed for the night in an incubator and flown by jet to Idaho Falls the next day. It was then taken by helicopter and jetboat to the sandhill crane nest at Grays Lake National Wildlife Refuge. The sandhill crane egg, on the other hand, was whisked away to the Patuxent Wildlife Research Center near Washington, D.C. There it is hatched and the chick raised, to be used in future experiments.

Intense study of the Rocky Mountain sandhill cranes made all of this possible. In the late 1960s and early '70s, Drewien and his colleagues began marking the sandhills at Grays Lake with colored leg bands. By constantly observing the cranes, the biologists learned the birds' migration routes, wintering areas and breeding habits. They observed the defense of territories, and they found that pairs returned to the same territories annually. They learned that the older, experienced cranes were more successful at raising young. And they found that the birds would tolerate considerable manipulation without abandoning their nests.

Whooping Crane Chick

These older, dependable sandhills are the ones chosen to incubate the Wood Buffalo whooping crane eggs. After they begin nesting in late April, Drewien locates the nests of prospective—often former—foster parents and monitors them throughout May. The sandhill cranes usually lay two eggs, but they will be given only one whooping crane egg. They might abandon their nest if they return to find one egg instead of two. So the biologists remove one of the sandhill eggs from each nest about a week before the whooping crane eggs arrive. If the foster parents abandon the single egg, it will not be a valuable whooping crane egg that is lost.

While the Americans are active in Idaho, Kuyt and his crew are just as busy in Canada, checking old established territories and searching for new ones. They monitor the progress of each pair throughout the summer, and band the young whoopers when they are nearly full grown. The banding of the birds has helped to greatly increase man's knowledge of the biology of whooping cranes. These birds, too, have considerable fidelity to their breeding territories. They return to the same areas each spring, probably until death. Some pairs have a long history of productivity, while others have seldom produced offspring. It has been hypothesized that one of the birds in unproductive pairs is reproductively impaired. In an effort to increase the number of young cranes reared at Wood Buffalo, an egg from a productive pair is sometimes placed in the nest of such a pair. All pairs are monitored for their own well-being as well as for the approaching egg transfer.

In late May half the whooping crane eggs are moved south, and crane lovers from both countries anxiously await the end of the 30-day incubation cycle. Unaware of all this outside interest, the young chicks, still in the eggs, develop in normal fashion. Siblings continue to grow but their eggs, once millimeters apart, are now separated by hundreds of miles. Late in the month each chick develops an egg tooth, a sharp protrusion on its bill which is used to break out of the shell.

When they emerge, the young whoopers are rusty brown and gangly. Both natural and foster parents take to them immediately. The adults brood them in the cold, teach them what to eat, and protect them from predators. The chicks will learn much from their parents during the next 8 to 11 months—if they survive that long.

All across North America and into Siberia similar scenes are occurring at thousands of crane nests. And in other nests the events are no less momentous. In Florida, Mississippi, and Cuba, nonmigratory subspecies of sandhill cranes—named after their respective areas—have a head start because of the southern climate. Their young are alrady several weeks old. There are an estimated 5,000 Florida cranes, but fewer than 150 Cuban cranes and only about 30 Mississippi sandhills. The Mississippi birds hang on to existence by an even thinner thread than do the whooping cranes, because their habitat is so limited.

There is a long and hazardous period before the young cranes begin to fly and can escape some of the dangers that may threaten them. It takes at least 60 days for the lesser sandhills to fledge, and sometimes whooping cranes require as much as 90 days.

Despite the different areas where the birds are hatched and raised, summer life is very similar for all crane chicks. The three major dangers which face all young cranes are exposure, starvation, and predators. The most critical period for the chicks is the first few weeks after hatching. During that time they are small and most susceptible to the cold and wet. The fuzzy down is not warm enough during cool nights or stormy weather. The parents and foster parents must brood the chicks until they have grown feathers and are able to regulate their own body temperatures. When several days of wet, cold weather have occurred while chicks are still small at Grays Lake, there have been significant losses among the foster whooping cranes. The same thing may also happen some years at Wood Buffalo National Park.

The young birds require large amounts of food to fuel their rapid growth from fuzzy chicks to full-

Whooping Crane Family at
Wood Buffalo National Park in Canada

sized cranes. The parents initially show or bring them food. The young learn quickly, however, and soon are adept at catching insects and—as they grow larger—frogs, minnows, and small birds as well.

Cold weather and drought are direct causes of starvation in crane chicks. The cold causes the small prey to go dormant. At Grays Lake, when the water level declines much of the marsh is left high and dry. That makes the marsh less productive and those years the survival rates of both whooping and sandhill crane chicks are lower. During five dry summers since the fostering project was begun, food shortages were at least partially responsible for poor fledging rates among the foster flock of whooping cranes.

Chicks that are weak or sick are also more susceptible to predation. Through the 1984 breeding season, 89 foster whooping cranes failed to reach the age of flight. Predators killed at least 23 and possibly as many as 58 of those young cranes. During the same period, 51 whooping cranes fledged.

Coyotes are the major predators at Grays Lake. They kill chicks and eat whooping crane eggs before they hatch. Although the weather and resulting conditions may kill more young cranes, something can be done about coyotes. The Fish and Wildlife Service began an active predator-control program in 1976 after it was clear that coyotes were a serious problem.

Black-necked Stilt

Golden eagles have also been known to prey on sandhill cranes and these birds of prey were also suspected in the disappearance of some foster whooping cranes there. Deer hunters in western Colorado observed one young whooper under attack by an eagle during migration in October 1979. The eagle dove on a flock of cranes, striking the young whooper which glided to the ground and died within 10 minutes.

Wolves are the major predator of flightless young whooping cranes at Wood Buffalo. At least six cases of wolves killing young whoopers have been documented during the last six years by Canadian biologists. Black bears have also been known to feast on whooper eggs, but during wet years it is difficult for either predator to reach nests or young cranes in the marshes.

Overall the Wood Buffalo whooping cranes have been doing a good job of producing offspring during the last decade. The removal of one egg from their nests has apparently not slowed their recovery. During two years, 1976 and 1977, they produced 22 young. Population growth was steady at six or seven chicks a year through 1983 except in 1981, when only two chicks reached Aransas. The new chicks fueled an increase in total breeding pairs. The 16 to 18 pairs found in the mid-70s has grown to 28 to 29 in the mid-80s. Their output has included 15 chicks in 1984, 16 in 1985 and as many as 20 chicks may arrive at Aransas during November of 1986. With any luck, the whooping crane count at Aransas may exceed 100 for the first time since the refuge was established. And these large numbers of chicks could swell the number of breeding pairs at Wood Buffalo in the early 1990s.

The number of whooping cranes at Grays Lake has also grown over the years. Through 1986, 265 whooping crane eggs have been placed in nests there (192 from Wood Buffalo, 73 from the captives in Patuxent). About 70 percent (187) of the eggs have hatched, and 82 chicks (31 percent) have fledged. In late August of 1986 about 30 of the whooping cranes were known to be alive.

Biologists hope that eventually the Rocky Mountain whooping cranes will reproduce, and although there are indications the birds will do so, they haven't yet. Every year since 1979 several adult males have returned to Grays Lake in the spring, established territories, and defended them against sandhills. But none of these males has had a mate.

The whoopers do realize they are different from the sandhills and tend to associate with each other. The great white cranes have been seen dancing together for short periods, and unison calling has also been observed. Most important of all was the apparent pairing of a young male and female during late summer of 1984 and throughout the breeding season of 1985. The two stayed together at Grays Lake, and in 1985 defended their territory against neighboring sandhills. They were seen dancing and unison calling. Their territory was far out in the marsh at Grays Lake, so it is unknown whether they built a nest or not. Since both birds were only three years old, it is doubtful that they could have laid fertile eggs. Whooping cranes are not sexually mature until they are four to six years old.

Nor was the pair bond strong: the two birds did not migrate or winter together. The potential was there; unfortunately, the female did not return to Grays Lake in the spring of 1986. It is not known whether she summered elsewhere or died after leaving the San Luis Valley.

Although some of the whooping cranes which are raised at Grays Lake return to the refuge each spring, many do not. They are found scattered throughout the northern Rockies. One favored summer haunt is the upper Green River Valley in Wyoming. But they have also been found in some very untraditional places. One subadult crane from the first group fostered by the sandhills spent its first two summers along the Green River in Utah, near the migration stopover at Ouray National Wildlife Refuge. However, he returned to Grays Lake during his third summer and established a territory the following summer. He returned to the territory and defended it each summer thereafter until his death in 1982.

Another whooper spent its first summer at Antero Reservoir, Colorado, only 130 miles north of the San Luis Valley. Perhaps the wisest yearling, one crane simply stayed in the San Luis Valley during its entire first summer. The bird saved itself a thousand miles of mountain travel in the process.

Northern Harrier (Marsh Hawk)

Though these wanderings are interesting, they do point out one of the major roadblocks preventing the formation of permanent pairs of whooping cranes within the Rocky Mountain flock. These whooping cranes are often miles from potential mates. Recent studies of pair bonding among whooping cranes at Aransas and of sandhill cranes in Florida show that it may take several years for the birds to develop a good, solid relationship. The subadult Aransas whooping cranes are found together much of the time both on the wintering grounds and in the Canadian marshlands during summer. The adults' nesting and wintering territories force the younger whoopers into habitat which is not being used by pairs or families. They spend a lot of time together and have the opportunity to associate with a number of possible mates.

The experimental flock of whooping cranes does not have that luxury. Although there are certain points where some whooping cranes concentrate, the whoopers are still scattered over two large areas during times when their Wood Buffalo–Aransas counterparts are more closely grouped. Normally, less than half of them are found at either Grays Lake or Bosque del Apache. Particulary in winter, there is not the social structure, the territorial system found at Aransas, to force them into subadult flocks of their own kind. Confounding the problem has been the tendency for the males to winter at the Bosque refuge and the known females to stay elsewhere in the Rio Grande Valley. Wherever they go they are mixed with the sandhills, like a few grains of salt in a sea of pepper.

A second problem has been apparent for some years. There are significantly more male cranes than females in the experimental flock. The reason for this is not known, but it makes it even harder for a territorial male to find a mate.

The biologists working with the experimental flock have decided to try to force the issue with the foster whoopers. During the summer of 1986, Rod Drewien and his crew captured several females summering in Wyoming and released them at Grays Lake, where several males were holding territories. No pairings developed immediately, but neither did the females fly back to Wyoming. Efforts to bring males and females together will continue.

Even if a few pairs of foster whooping cranes begin to breed in the late 1980s, it will take more time to build up a self-sustaining population at Grays Lake. The goal is to have 25 breeding pairs there. Biometricians at the University of Idaho are currently analyzing the time that might be required to reach this goal. Meanwhile, eggs will continue to be flown south for hatching at Grays Lake.

Aircraft are also important in another phase of the Idaho crane project. When it's time to band the young birds, just before they start to fly, they must be captured. At first Drewien ran them down on foot, but some foster parents became increasingly difficult to approach and hid their chicks in dense vegetation. Since 1976, a helicopter has been used to scour the marsh and capture as many chicks as possible. The helicopter flies low over the chick, allowing Drewien to leap to the marsh and grab it before it can run away and hide.

It is handled quickly. The chick's weight is recorded, measurements are taken and it is banded within minutes. Since 1978, foster whooper chicks have had radio transmitters attached to their leg bands, and these have been invaluable in tracking the birds through the first few years of their lives.

This capture technique—tried and tested first on sandhill cranes, then on foster whoopers at Grays Lake—has also been used since 1977 to capture chicks at Wood Buffalo for marking.

Courting Western Grebes

By late August or early September, most of the young cranes at Grays Lake have begun to fly. The families abandon their territories and join subadult flocks and other families. They forage together in grain fields during the day and roost together in the marshes at night. This is "staging," the premigration activity which prepares the birds for the first leg of fall migration. Through September the number of cranes at Grays Lake grows. The birds from surrounding areas are feeling the same impulses as their on-refuge kin.

Grays Lake is only one of about 10 important staging areas for the cranes of the Rocky Mountains. They also come together at a half-dozen other places in eastern Idaho and on the lower Bear and the Salt rivers in Wyoming. Each area has many things in common, like grain fields for feeding and marshy roosts for the nights.

In late September there are usually several thousand sandhills at Grays Lake, and all the whooping cranes which have summered or been raised there that year. Groups of several thousand each have also gathered at the other Idaho and Wyoming staging areas. The fall air is beginning to clear the haze of summer. It is crisp, and something triggers a familiar response in the great birds of the northern marshes. As October approaches the cranes begin to spiral up into the sky in midmorning. They are again testing the wind and their strength. Their cries are heard throughout the valleys where they have congregated.

Then one morning it happens. The wind is coming from the north or northwest. The sky is clear, and instead of returning to the Idaho and

Wyoming marshes, the sandhills and whoopers strike out for another familiar place—the San Luis Valley of southern Colorado.

The route is similar to the one taken during the spring migration north. Below them, people cutting firewood and clearing fields take a few minutes to listen. As if their own calendars haven't made it clear enough, these passing birds impress upon them just how near winter is.

By October there are few cranes left at Grays Lake. Even Rod Drewien has moved south to the San Luis Valley. He moves at the birds' pace, following a signal from a single whooping crane's transmitter. One family he tracked took three days to reach the San Luis Valley. The birds stopped the first night on the Henry's Fork in southwestern Wyoming. The second night was spent in a mountain meadow at 9,000 feet on the side of Colorado's Grand Mesa. On the afternoon of the third day the cranes arrived at the San Luis Valley. They had traveled 120 miles the first day and about 180 on each succeeding day. Other families have made the jump in just two days, spending the night at Ouray National Wildlife Refuge in Utah, 210 miles from Grays Lake. The remaining 275 miles were covered the following day, and the birds arrived at the San Luis Valley about an hour after dark.

Although most subadult whooping cranes migrate through the San Luis Valley, a few have wandered east of the Rocky Mountains. One whooper stopped briefly in northeastern Colorado during the fall of 1979. Two more stopped there in the fall of 1985. They stayed there for six weeks, one 40 miles southeast of the other. One lone crane stopped off at Las Vegas National Wildlife Refuge on the plains of eastern New Mexico on his way to the Rio Grande. He then returned to the same locales in the spring of 1986. Apparently he prefers to travel around the Colorado Rockies.

Most of the foster whooping cranes continue to follow the migration route taught to them by their greater sandhill crane parents. They join thousands of the grey cranes during migration, and are becoming familiar sights in the marshes and sandbar roosts their cousins have been using for thousands of years.

Concerns

The coyote loped casually along the irrigation ditch, his thick gray fur showing he was well insulated against winter. In the corn field, where hundreds of cranes and snow geese fed, his passing did not go unnoticed. The prairie wolf's pace quickened and without warning he darted toward the flock. The geese leapt into the air, but a weak one faltered, stumbling as it turned and tried to fly. The coyote swerved, pouncing upon the hapless bird, driving it to the ground.

A white cloud of geese erupted. Honking wildly, they filled the skies over the north end of the Bosque del Apache tour loop, to the delight of spectators.

Before the coyote—dragging the goose—had disappeared into brush surrounding the field, the geese were returning to continue their feeding. Some birds failed to even lift off during the attack. Perhaps they, too, were too weak or too ill to struggle with the wind on this cloudy day.

In 1985 the snow goose population along the Rio Grande peaked at about 70,000 birds. There were also 25,000 sandhill cranes and thousands of mallards, Canada geese, and other waterfowl. Bosque del Apache alone had 57,000 snow geese and 15,000 sandhill cranes.

With all those birds jammed into a valley which is steadily being turned into mobile home lots and housing developments, problems can be expected. Snow geese collected by the New Mexico Department of Game and Fish in February of 1986 showed signs of strain. The birds had prominent breastbones and no body fat. Their breast muscles were weak from a winter of poor feeding, and they were in poor condition for the migration north. In fact, 3,000 geese died at the Banks Island nesting colony in the western Arctic in the spring of 1986. Unseasonably late ice and snow still covered the island when the birds arrived, and they were too weak to stay alive until winter finally broke. Those birds are believed to have wintered in New Mexico.

In addition to starvation, large flocks of wild birds face other threats. Fowl cholera becomes more of a problem when birds are crowded or during weather-related stress. The loss of wetlands, such as the one that occurred in the Rainwater Basin in south-central Nebraska, congregates the birds too closely. In the basin, only 9,000 acres of marsh remain of the original 94,000 acres. As many as 75,000 birds have died there during dry years when they were crowded together and cholera struck.

Cholera has killed ducks, geese, and cranes at Bosque del Apache. At least one whooping crane was infected. It was captured by biologists, and was recovering from the disease at the Rio Grande Zoo in Albuquerque when it broke its leg and subsequently died of shock during an operation.

Another disease that threatens the whooping cranes is avian tuberculosis (TB). Two of the white cranes died of TB during the spring of 1986. TB is a chronic disease. While birds with cholera usually die quickly, the health of those with TB declines

Whooping Cranes in Flight

gradually. They can die from other causes, such as predation or a collision, because of their weakened condition. A third whooper, found dead beside a powerline in Idaho in April of 1986, also had symptoms of tuberculosis. Before 1986, TB had claimed only one whooper; that death occurred in the San Luis Valley in 1982. The rise in cases is very significant, because 10 percent of the 30 Rocky Mountain whooping cranes were stricken with the disease, and a poor production year at Grays Lake failed to replace those birds within the flock.

Clearly, something needs to be done to minimize the risk of starvation and disease. One alternative is to expand Bosque del Apache National Wildlife Refuge, increasing the amount of agricultural land devoted to grain production for the birds. This would be an expensive proposition, however, and with shrinking budgets forecast for the Fish and Wildlife Service, it is an unlikely program as well.

Hunting, it has been thought, could help reduce these threats to all the birds by dispersing them over a wider area. Goose hunting has been allowed at the Bosque refuge since the 1960s. In recent years, as the numbers of geese and cranes wintering there have climbed, biologists have tried to use hunters to push some of the geese farther south.

But the arrival of whooping cranes on the refuge in 1975 changed the situation. It was important that the endangered whoopers be protected. So biologists have tried to balance the needs of the whooping cranes with the need to disperse the geese and the desire of hunters to hunt geese. Since 1975, goose hunters at Bosque del Apache have been required to attend a course in waterfowl identification before hunting. The course takes about two hours and introduces the hunters to the various types of birds which occur on the refuge. The slides shown illustrate the differences between whooping cranes and snow geese, and the hunters must pass a test at the end of the class. If a person fails, he will not be allowed to hunt on the refuge that year. This has resulted in a very safe hunt at the Bosque refuge. No whooping cranes have been shot in 11 years, and the number of illegally killed Canada geese, white-fronted geese, and sandhill cranes has been reduced through the hunter-education course.

Whooping Crane

Still, the goose hunt has come under great scrutiny, because it may be having a negative effect on the foster whooping crane project. Dr. Rod Drewien is among the biologists who believe hunting the fields of the refuge is disturbing the whooping cranes during the winter, a critical period in the pair bonding process.

Sandhill crane numbers have also increased since the 1960s. As the numbers of cranes and geese have grown, private landowners have complained about the damage by these birds to their crops. To combat growing discontent among farmers, the first sandhill crane hunt in the Middle Rio Grande Valley since the signing of the Migratory Bird Treaty Act of 1916 was held in October of 1986. A limited number of crane hunting permits—730—was available as much to chase some birds out of the valley as to harvest them.

Game managers felt that the hunt would have minimal effects on the whooping cranes. Crane hunters also had to pass the identification course in order to participate, and the hunt was held when most of the sandhills and whooping cranes were still in the San Luis Valley. Crane hunting was not allowed on the Bosque refuge or on the nearby state waterfowl areas, and the hunt plan included closure of any part of the valley if a whooping crane took up residence there.

Whooping cranes in the naturally occurring flock at Aransas National Wildlife Refuge do not have this human factor to contend with. The only hunting on the Texas refuge is for deer and feral hogs, and those hunts are not in the marshes used by the cranes. But the whoopers of Aransas also have thousands of years of tradition bringing them to these coastal marshes. As evidenced by their wintering in such a limited portion of the apparently available habitat, their genetic coding may be very specific when it comes to winter activities.

The whooping cranes of the Rocky Mountains may have the same genes, but they do not have a rich tradition of association with their winter homeland. Everything is new for this flock of 30 birds, and they may need greater stability at Bosque del Apache for them to actually begin the critical bonding which could result in reproduction.

Hunting itself is a controversial activity for a wildlife refuge. Many people feel that the purpose of refuges, as the name implies, is to protect wildlife—especially endangered species. Hunting on the Bosque refuge may be eroding support from a large segment of the public that does not wish to see dead or crippled geese along the tour loop or birds being shot from the sky.

Hunters, too, understand the value of protecting diminishing wildlife. They have supported legislation that makes them pay taxes on firearms and ammunition, buy state hunting licenses, and purchase federal Duck Stamps to support state and federal wildlife management programs. They have seen those monies used to pay for National Wildlife Refuges, and have always been allowed to hunt on a portion of these refuge lands they helped to buy. Most support the efforts to save the whooping crane and other endangered species while still wanting an opportunity to pursue their sport.

So biologists and managers continue to search for a solution. Because there are so many birds, people, and opinions involved, finding the best answer is difficult. The effort in 1986 was two-pronged. The goose hunt on Bosque refuge was limited to four 2- or 3-day periods in November. Geese were hunted in the marshes during midday as they returned to drink and rest. This time was chosen because most of the cranes, including the whoopers, remain in the fields all day. This compromise allowed hunters to pursue their sport while limiting disturbance of whooping cranes. Some geese were chased from the refuge. Bird watchers were inconvenienced by the closure of the tour loop during hunting hours. The whooping cranes were not troubled by hunting for the remainder of the winter, providing them an opportunity to seek out suitable mates.

The second part of the 1986 management plan was an effort to disperse the geese from the Bosque refuge by limiting their access to the corn in the fields. Until 1986 the Fish and Wildlife Service knocked down all the corn so that it was accessible to both geese and cranes. During the winter of 1986–87 the ears were knocked down, but the corn stalks were left standing. Geese are less likely to feed in standing corn, because they cannot see approaching predators. Refuge personnel also disturbed flocks of snow geese from airboats with flashing mirrors and other passive means of harassment.

The results of these management efforts will be continually evaluated, but the welfare of the whooping crane, since it is an endangered species, will always be one of the most important factors in this decision-making process.

Disease, disturbance, and a lack of breeding pairs are not the only problems faced by the Rocky Mountain whooping cranes. They have also had a higher mortality rate than those of the natural flock. Man-made structures have claimed a significant number of the foster whooping cranes. Five are known to have died after striking or becoming entangled in barbed-wire fences. Nine more have died or been severely injured in collisions with powerlines. Most of the wire strikes have occurred during periods of poor light, early or late in the day, or in foggy or stormy weather. And most have occurred in the San Luis Valley or on the summering grounds in Idaho and Wyoming.

Five whooping cranes in the Wood Buffalo–Aransas flock have also died after hitting powerlines. All of these deaths have happened during migration, one on the Canadian prairie and four in Texas and Kansas locations where the birds had stopped overnight.

After recognizing the powerline hazard, the U.S. Fish and Wildlife Service aggressively investigated new powerline proposals, trying to route them away from marshes and feeding areas the birds use. They have required the placement of markers, usually large orange balls, on lines in areas where the risk of crane collisions is high. The electrical industry has also actively participated by conducting some studies and cooperating in others.

The Aransas flock of whooping cranes is also threatened by chemical and oil spills along the Gulf Intracoastal Waterway, which runs through the middle of the cranes' wintering area. Some people have suggested rerouting the waterway outside the refuge, a costly proposal.

The biggest threat to North America's cranes is the loss of habitat. Indeed, this is the greatest danger to the survival of all wildlife throughout the world. In the cranes' case, the Platte River provides the most vivid example of what we are doing to nature.

For centuries the plains of what is now called Nebraska were home each spring to migrating sandhill and whooping cranes. There were miles upon miles of marshes and meadows. Today there are miles upon miles of grain fields. The marshes have been drained, and even the mighty river has been changed significantly.

Before settlement of the plains, the Platte was a wide, free-flowing river of the grasslands. Today it is lined with trees, which were all but absent just 150 years ago. The Platte used to flood each spring as the snows melted upstream. The resulting sediments and flowing ice scoured the riverbed, uprooting saplings and leveling islands and sandbars which were trying to establish themselves along the channel. Periodic summer fires also helped to limit the distribution of trees. In 1840, when the pioneers were arriving, the Platte was "a mile wide and an inch deep, too thick to drink, to thin to plow." It was a haven for the migrating cranes. The river was a perfect roost, and food was abundant in nearby wet meadows and buffalo wallows.

With settlement came changes. First the wildfires were controlled, then the river. Water was too valuable a resource to remain in a streambed. The first dams were built in the early 1900s on the North Platte in Wyoming. More followed on the South Platte in Colorado. Kingsley Dam, the biggest on the Platte system, was built in the 1940s. It backed up the North Platte for 30 miles in western Nebraska. Large canals were constructed to carry the water to outlying reservoirs and farms.

The Platte became meeker. It could no longer flood and scour itself clean in the spring. Trees took hold on islands and gradually the river was forced into increasingly narrower channels. Part of its flows seeped downward to replenish the underground aquifer that was being pumped to irrigate surrounding fields.

Today, 70 percent of the Platte's annual flow is diverted. The cranes which once had a long, mile-wide river for roosting are being concentrated in much smaller areas every year. The Audubon Society and the Whooping Crane Habitat Trust have been forced to bulldoze trees and other vegetation to try to maintain the roosts found on their property in the Big Bend region.

As if that's not enough, government and private agencies are trying to claim the last 30 percent of the Platte. They propose substitute roosts for the cranes, but once the flow has been reduced even further, how long will it take for the trees to claim it altogether? The agencies say they'll bulldoze dikes to create suitable roosts, but when the budget restrictions hit will the wildlife money be the first to be cut? The only safe answer is to reserve the remaining flows for cranes and other wildlife. That will mean a hard fight for conservationists; proposed projects will have to be defeated and laws will have to be changed. The Platte is extremely important to sandhill cranes. It would be a shameful example of man's greed if the "Crane River" were lost forever.

Despite the Platte's importance, other wetlands are also significant. Radio-tracking of whooping cranes across the Great Plains showed that the great white birds often used small, isolated marshes and stock ponds for overnight stops. Biologist Gary Lingle of the Whooping Crane Habitat Trust argues that these sites are not what the cranes would choose, but what they have been forced into by the loss of thousands of acres of wetlands. The majority of the marshes found on the continent when Europeans first arrived have vanished, and the flights of waterfowl which blackened the sky have likewise diminished.

Cranes throughout the world are experiencing the same problems as those in North America. Of the 15 species of cranes found in the world, more than a third are considered vulnerable or endangered. The whooping crane reached the lowest level of any crane population when it bottomed out at 21 in 1941. In fact, all whooping cranes in the wild or in captivity (about 185 in 1986) have come from the 15 birds living at Aransas in 1941. The six whoopers in Louisiana in 1941 died without further reproduction. The whoopers have shown significant progress, but the road ahead is still a big question mark. Can the birds overcome their strict social structure and use more of the available habitat at Aransas, or will disease strike them? Will enough habitat be saved to maintain their existence in the years ahead? Will the Rocky Mountain whooping crane flock be capable of reproducing without continued manipulation by man?

The Rocky Mountain crane flock is of interest to crane watchers and biologists throughout the world. If the experiment succeeds here, it could be applied to other species which are in trouble.

The failure of cranes to pair during 11 years of the experiment is a cloud over the project. Their limited numbers and wide-ranging habits make it hard to determine if they will finally produce their own young. There is no doubt they recognize each other, and are willing to associate with their own kind. The survival of the cranes beyond five years of age is critical. Only five birds older than five were in the foster flock in the summer of 1986, whereas in the Wood Buffalo–Aransas flock at least 14 color-banded birds of like ages are members of breeding pairs. Causes of death among free-flying foster whooping cranes have included diseases, eagles, heart failure, fence and powerline injuries and even lead poisoning (one crane ate a camera battery). But only 44 percent of the deaths of whooping cranes which have fledged at Grays Lake can be explained. The other 56 percent are unknowns and may spell serious trouble for the cranes. Some of these cranes have undoubtedly succumbed to the known causes, but is there some other major source of crane mortality that has not yet been identified? Biologists must continue to seek out mortality factors and work to limit or eliminate their effects.

The evaluation of the experimental whooping crane program will continue, and scrutiny will probably intensify. The eggs available for experiments are increasing as the Wood Buffalo–Aransas flock grows. Eggs are needed to replenish the flock held at Patuxent and to start a second captive flock. Some Canadians would like to keep eggs in Canada to start a new foster flock there. Other ideas being considered include starting sedentary flocks of whooping cranes, and studies are being done of the nonmigratory flocks of sandhills in Florida and Georgia to see if they would be suitable foster parents for other whoopers. These sandhills nest too early to receive Wood Buffalo eggs, but a captive flock could be manipulated to produce eggs earlier. "Gentle release" of captive reared whoopers is also being considered for these areas, since sedentary birds would not need to learn migration routes from foster parents. This technique, developed for the endangered Mississippi sandhill crane, allows captive-reared yearlings to gradually acclimate to wild surroundings, first in a pen and then in the vicinity of that pen.

Perhaps the nonmigratory approach will prove to be most successful. With more powerlines stretching across the country each year the hazards of migration may become a risk this endangered species cannot afford. With marshes being drained each year a dependable supply of water will become an important consideration of any effort to establish another wild flock.

Sandhill and whooping cranes face some formidable problems. Preserving a place for them is going to be a major task requiring large amounts of resources and imagination. The whooping crane projects, past and present, stand as tributes to the men and women who love wild things. These efforts to preserve a species which once was so close to the brink of extenction should all be regarded with great respect. The imagination used by men to try to solve the cranes' problems has been remarkable. But the job is not done.

Our forefathers eliminated a species which once filled the skies, the passenger pigeon. Through ignorance and greed a valuable part of the world was forever lost to us.

However, there have been many success stories in wildlife management in this century. Antelope, wild turkey, white-tailed deer, and trumpeter swans have all returned from very diminished numbers. The successes have been great, but this is no time to stop. The greatest success story of all, that of the whooping crane, is yet to be completed.

References

The scientific reports on cranes number in the thousands. Of particular assistance in the preparation of this book were the following proceedings, papers, and books:

Allen, R. P. 1952. "The whooping crane." *National Audubon Society*, Research Report 3. 246 pages.

Bishop, M. A. 1984. "The dynamics of subadult flocks of whooping cranes wintering in Texas, 1978–79 through 1982–83." M.S. Thesis, Texas A&M University, College Station, Texas. 128 pages.

Currier, P. J., G. R. Lingle, and J. G. VanDerwalker. 1985. *Migratory bird habitat on the Platte and North Platte Rivers in Nebraska.* The Platte River Whooping Crane Critical Habitat Maintenance Trust, Grand Island, Nebraska. 177 pages.

Drewien, R. C. and E. G. Bizeau. 1974. "Status and distribution of greater sandhill cranes in the Rocky Mountains." *Journal of Wildlife Management*, 38: 720–742.

Drewien, R. C. and E. G. Bizeau. 1977. "Cross-fostering whooping cranes to sandhill crane foster parents." Pages 201–222 in *Endangered Birds: Management Techniques for Preserving Threatened Species*, S. A. Temple, Editor. The University of Wisconsin Press, Madison, Wisconsin. 466 pages.

Drewien, R. C. and E. Kuyt. 1979. "Teamwork Helps the Whooping Crane." *National Geographic*, 155: 680–693.

Drewien, R. C., S. H. Bouffard, D. D. Call, and R. A. Wonacott. 1985. "The whooping crane cross-fostering experiment: the role of animal damage control." Paper presented at Second Eastern Wildlife Damage Control Conference. Raleigh, North Carolina.

Johnsgard, P. A. 1982. *Cranes of the World.* Indiana University Press, Bloomington, Indiana. 257 pages.

Lewis, J. C., Editor. 1979. *Proceedings: 1975 Crane Workshop.* 40 scientific papers on cranes. Oklahoma State University Publishing and Printing, Stillwater, Oklahoma. 355 pages.

Lewis, J. C., Editor. 1979. *Proceedings: 1978 Crane Workshop.* 36 scientific papers on cranes. Colorado State University Printing Service, Fort Collins, Colorado. 259 pages.

Lewis, J. C., Editor. 1982. *Proceedings: 1981 Crane Workshop.* 39 scientific papers on cranes. National Audubon Society, Tavenier, Florida. 296 pages.

Lewis, J. C., Editor. 1986 (at press). *Proceedings: 1985 Crane Workshop.* 53 scientific papers on cranes. Platte River Whooping Crane Critical Habitat Maintenance Trust, Grand Island, Nebraska.

Lewis, J. C. 1986. "The Whooping Crane." Pages 659–676 in *Audubon Wildlife Report 1986,* R. L. DiSilvestro, Editor. National Audubon Society, New York, New York. 1094 pages.

Lewis, J. C., and H. Masotomi, Editors. 1981. *Crane Research Around the World.* 48 scientific papers on cranes. International Crane Foundation, Baraboo, Wisconsin. 286 pages.

Walkinshaw, L. H. 1973. *Cranes of the World.* Winchester Press, New York, New York. 370 pages.

Whooping Crane Recovery Team. 1986 (at press). *Whooping Crane Recovery Plan.* U.S. Fish and Wildlife Service, Albuquerque, New Mexico. 200 pages.

Whooping Crane *Canadian Sandhill Crane* *Greater Sandhill Crane* *Lesser Sandhill Crane*

	Height	Weight	Wingspan
Whooping Crane	57″	11–16 lbs.	87″
Greater Sandhill Crane	48″	9–13 lbs.	72″
Canadian Sandhill Crane	42″	7–11 lbs.	66″
Lesser Sandhill Crane	39″	6– 8 lbs.	60″

DIFFERENT SPECIES AND SUBSPECIES OF NORTH AMERICAN CRANES

	Scientific Name	Common Name
	Grus americana	whooping crane There are no recognized subspecies of whooping cranes.
	Grus canadensis tabida	greater sandhill crane There are five separate populations of greater sandhill cranes, each nesting and wintering apart from the other populations. The Rocky Mountain population is one of these.
Migratory subspecies	G. c. *canadensis*	lesser sandhill crane
	G. c. *rowani*	Canadian sandhill crane
Nonmigratory subspecies	G. c. *pratensis*	Florida sandhill crane
	G. c. *pulla*	Mississippi sandhill crane
	G. c. *nesiotes*	Cuban sandhill crane

About the Authors

Dale Stahlecker is a wildlife biologist with Eagle Ecological Services. He has bachelor's and master's degrees from Colorado State University. Dale has worked for several federal agencies, both as an employee and a consultant, and has consulted for a variety of agencies and interests since moving to New Mexico in 1980. He grew up in the San Luis Valley, has studied cranes on the Platte River in Nebraska, and has recently been monitoring crane migration in northern New Mexico.

Martin Frentzel is an outdoor writer whose work has appeared in the *Albuquerque Journal* for 10 years. He has lived in New Mexico most of his life, and his family moved to White Rock in the mid-1960s. He first became interested in cranes from watching the large birds migrating over the family home.

LisaBeth Daly grew up in Albuquerque, New Mexico. An artist since an early age, she studied art at Oberlin College in Ohio. She taught art in North Carolina before returning to Albuquerque where she currently draws, paints, and operates a graphic design firm.

Mallard